Jesus
at the
Bottom of a Coffee Cup

Poems, prayers, and reflections from
a woman in her twenties.

Malinda Lugbill

Illustrated by: Claire Wiest

ISBN 979-8-88943-838-0 (paperback)
ISBN 979-8-88943-839-7 (digital)

Christian Faith Publishing
832 Park Avenue
Meadville, PA 16335
www.christianfaithpublishing.com

Printed in the United States of America

Author Note

Poetry has always been a way for me to connect to God, to process life through creative prayer, by putting a pen to paper and just writing. I always said my poetry would be a private endeavor, a creation of the heart between me and God. But then, I was convicted to publish my story. This is my story through poetry, prayers, and scripture reflections. This is my journey about learning to surrender my heart to the Lord in every season of my life, especially in the seasons of waiting and growth. This is my story of anxiety in a world pandemic, in a constant battle with comparison, and time through graduate school. This is my story of conversations with myself, my best friends, family, ex-boyfriends, acquaintances, and strangers. Conversations with the Heavenly Father through desperate prayer. Many a conversation happened over a solid cup of coffee, and when I reached the end of the coffee cup, there was more than just a coffee stain at the bottom—my heart was full of inspiration and creativity because of the conversations. This is my story about how God speaks through His creation and speaks to my heart when I am nearest the water and His beauty.

Surrender is difficult, and if you are in a season of change, growth, and long waiting—you are not alone.

Prologue

I'm scared.
To respond.
To put out there
Words
That hold weight in my life

And could hold weight
In someone else's

Heart

Of God.
That's what I'm after.

Obedience, too.
Let me be faithful in a calling
I'm scared to follow.

Use my words.
Let them be
Yours.

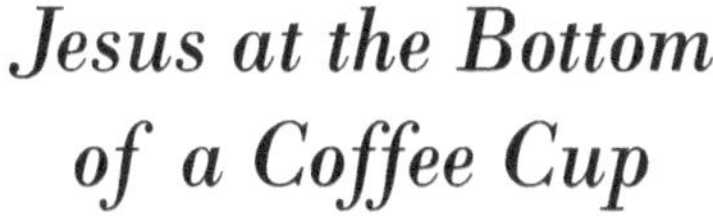

Jesus at the Bottom
of a Coffee Cup

Where the sugar sinks to the bottom,
Dark splotches linger on a stark white
Ceramic canvas,
The warm, cozy feeling once enclosed inside,
Now coating the heart
Of the beholder

But at the bottom of that ceramic canvas,
Leftover sugar isn't the only sweetness one will find,
Nor just residue from the
Pick-me-up liquid

But one can find
Jesus
At the bottom of the coffee mug
So sweet, a lingering Presence
Who makes Himself known
Through conversations
And availability
Through consistency, accountability,
And pursuit

In the bottom of the coffee cup
Although the coffee is sipped, gone

Jesus isn't.

And He continues to fill the hearts
Of the beholders of the
Ceramic canvas

The Example

You gave us Your Spirit
So that we might live
a gospel-centered life
But what does that look like?

Jesus.

Emptied Himself in
Humility,
Lived as a human
Not focused on offending
But on loving
Died
In obedience
Out of love
To extend grace

Silence.

Then with victory
Resurrection
Life

So, Lord,
Give me eyes to see the broken
Ears to listen to the unheard voices
And a selfless heart
To extend grace
Just like Your Son,

Jesus.

Dorm 121

The sticky stars on my ceiling glow in the dark
I lie awake with so many thoughts
Why are my hips so big?
Will any man love me?
(*Probably not*) an echo in my head responds
What will my future be like?

But you, God, are not of this world
You probably smile an empathetic smile
And say,
"Little do you know, child—
Wait.
Wait and see the things
I AM doing."

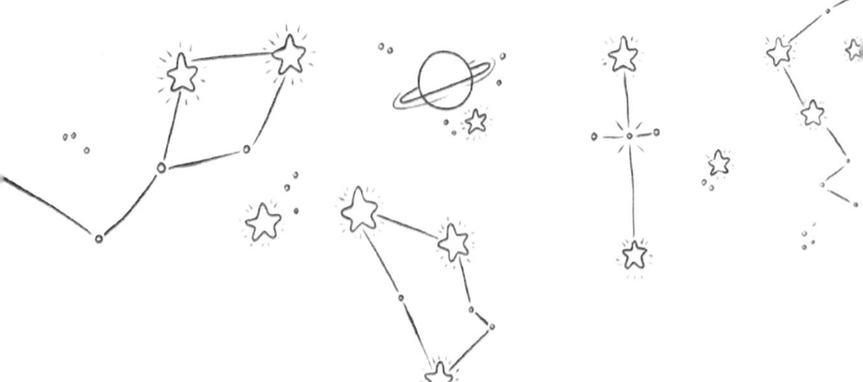

Rooted

Although today I am moving
Let my heart be rooted in You
Although the world is constantly
Changing
Remind me that You are
Constant
Although the world is so broken
Make beauty out of ashes
Although society is constructed
In a manner where the color of our skin wins,
Remind us that we are
All sinners
That we are
All children
Of You
Our Father of Truth
Although I may feel lonely in the midst of
Chaos
Remind me that You
Never leave
And that
Nothing
Absolutely nothing
Can separate me from Your love

Click

Click.
It's out of my hands
It's in Yours, Lord.

Fear, instant fear.

What if I'm not good enough?
What if I am inadequate?
What if I didn't do something
Perfectly?

My heart pounds,
I stare at the screen,
One click,
And it's out of my hands
It's in yours now, Lord.

Calm my heart,
Replace my fear
With joy,
Replace my fear
With trust.

One click
And it's out of my hands
One life; my life
Let it be in Your hands.

Seamless Devotion

The sun is warm on my face
It sparkles across the cool gray surface of the water
As the water flows
Seamlessly,
Smoothly
Let my heart do the same
Let it be
Undivided
Let my thoughts
My actions
My words
My worship
My motivation
Be devoted to You
Alone
Seamlessly
Smoothly
Let my heart sing like the birds

Believing Your Truth
And not lies

Like Ruth
(Ruth 3:5–11)

"Lord,
Let my heart be loyal to you.
Let my heart be united so that it seeks nothing
That is attractive and glittering
From the world
But let my heart seek You alone,
In obedience."

Ducks

The waves come
All at once
But the ducks just glide
They move with the waves
Embracing them
Let me be like the ducks
Gliding with the waves
Knowing that
You
Are the only One Who can calm them
Who can reveal my weeds
Reveal to me the areas of neglect
Let me tend to them
And let Your grace
Make my brokenness
Whole

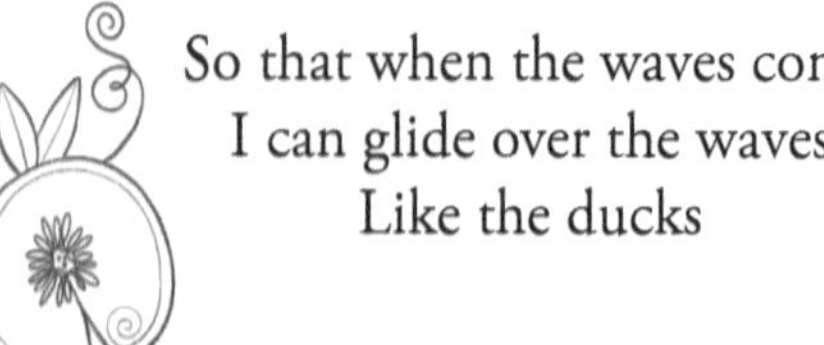

So that when the waves come
I can glide over the waves
Like the ducks

Apartment A

In this space,
In this small apartment
Meet us here, meet me here
Holy Spirit, invade my heart
Invade this space
Fill us with boldness
So that in every area
Of my life
My communities
Will feel Your Presence

While I sit here
Waiting in the silence
Let Your Spirit invade
This space, this apartment,
My heart.
So that everyone I encounter
Will feel You close
Will be filled with boldness
To trust
To obey
And to further Your Kingdom
To hope in You
Alone

Ghost Town

The only sound was the
Echo
Of my own footsteps in the street
I like it better

The way things were before

When the streets were crowded
Lives were busy, and society was
On the move
But what we didn't know was

The roles of the ghost town were reversed

When the world came to a halt
When the streets were emptied
And homes were full
The grocery aisles were cleared
But our pantries stocked
What we didn't know was that

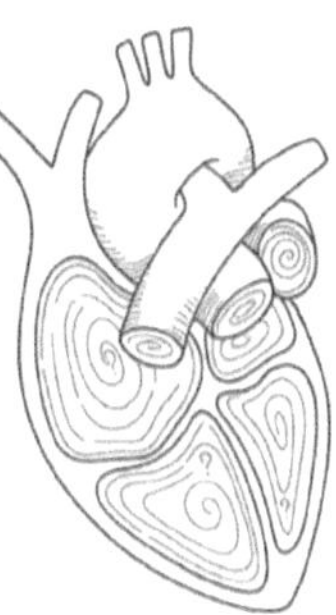

The way things were before

Our hearts were empty
Searching
For something more
The only sound in our hearts was

The cry for help

Was loud
Obnoxious
But we were able to ignore it
Filling our lives with meaningless
Fillers

Distractions

Now gone.
The world around us
Silent
A ghost town
But our hearts

Active

With the living God
He is working in the ghost town of hearts
By silencing everything else

Blue Polyester

Maybe we were wearing masks
The whole time
Maybe the smiles on our faces
Were plastered
Hiding the fact that our hearts
Were unsettled
Were searching
Hitchhiking onto any earthly pleasure
That seemed promising

But now we are wearing masks
And the complaints are rising
Maybe we are beginning to realize that we
Were wearing a mask
The whole time

And now we are truly tired of it
The physical masks we wear don't work as well
They don't hide our
Fears and anxieties
In fact
They amplify them

You can see it in the eyes
The silent cry for help

Built for Freedom

We were built for the
Creator
To love Him, serve Him,
Point to Him.

But we try to follow our own
Deceptive hearts.
We think we were built to
Live independently

To be free

And we are…
But not in the way we think.
In our minds, independence means
Control.
Freedom means individuality.

But we were built for the
Creator,
Who made us as individuals
But calls us to be
Unified

So that we may love Him
Serve Him, point to Him
And heed His Spirit's calling
In the midst of the loud world

There is freedom in surrender

Open Heart Posture

Infiltrate my heart
Let the warmth that slowly spreads
Disperse rapidly throughout my body
Let my ears always be tuned
To the soft sound of the water
Let my eyes always notice
What is not visible

To the one that is in bondage
Let the posture of my heart
Be free
Infiltrate my heart

Proverbs 12:11

Worthless pursuits,
Instagram, money, acceptance,
People-pleasing, success,
All end in death
In disappointment
In the inability to follow your first love

But working the land,
Improving the heart,
Clearing the weeds,
Choosing to follow God
Even when it feels unsafe
There,
Bread will be given
Life.
Love, fruitful growth, light.
Because you are a faithful worker,
The Kingdom will be furthered
And that
Is my only goal
To live with the Kingdom mindset and heart
To follow my first love

Stillness
(Psalm 46:10 ESV)

Deep dark blue
Wispy white gentle
Smooth clear glass below

Bright blue
Warm sun reflecting
Same smooth clear glass

Lord, You are creative
You are active
Show me how I can delight in You
How every moment can be given
Back to You.

Thank You for Your grace
For Your love
For Your peace.
Let us delight in You today because You say,
"Be still and know."

Why, God?

I feel you calling me to stop asking
Why
And do everything out of obedience
And love for you

Isn't that enough?

Dancing in a Parking Lot

Intricate colors,
Each one distinct but blending with the whole,
Intricate movements,
Each body, each limb in time with
the music in a different way,
Each heart soaking in the way God moves

It's funny how airports
Airport parking lots
Can hold the Presence of the Holy Spirit
So plainly

The night sky dark, but the moon, stars,
And lights in our eyes
Illuminated the parking lot
Intricate movements
Captured the way
You moved, God,
And will continue to move

It's funny how airports
Signify going places,
But in that moment
I knew You,

God,
Weren't going anywhere
You weren't
Aren't
Done yet.

First Day Jitters
(*Philippians 4:6 ESV*)

"Do not be anxious about anything"

I was just a scared freshman
Searching for community
For acceptance
For my niche
In a new home

But pray about everything

Now here I sit
Community found
Niche settled into
Home

A senior, grad student
First day
Twenty-two years old

But I feel ten
Ready for the first day
Jitters inside my belly

It's funny how the first day
Makes you feel young again
But excited to move on

To keep doing Kingdom work
As a student
As a future employee
As myself
As a child of God.

him

I pray for him
Widen his heart, open his eyes
Let him see what You are doing
Fill him with an overwhelming peace
To trust Your timing, Your plan.

I pray for his heart,
Tune it in to listen to Your Spirit
Let love grow deep roots so that
Gardens grow and provide for
Everyone he comes in contact with.

I pray for his health
Mental, physical, spiritual
Give his mind, body, and heart
A sense of peace
Knowing that he is a temple for You

I pray for Your timing,
Whoever it may be, let us both
Trust You

Prepare my heart
Prepare his
Ultimately
Be the foundation

You, Always

It is not me.
It's never been me
It is You.

No one
Can make a beautiful body of
water reflect the gray sky,
The crisp air leaves a refreshing chill
and a purple color on my fingers
The green grass bright against the
Dull reflective water

Except You.
It has always been You.

No one
Can fill a heart with so much peace
With so much joy and freedom

Can speak so softly in the chaos
Can pursue in love so fiercely

Except You.
It has always been You.

Agape

"Soon, my beloved"
Until then, let the posture of
my heart be open-faced
Toward You
Don't let me waste this wait
In this season, let my desire be You.

But if I have doubt,
Use it to bring me close
If my heart is tangled in an overwhelmed state,
Give me space
Small moments
To experience Your goodness
If I choose to take a path
That does not align with Yours
Realign my heart

All in all, let the posture of my heart
be open-faced toward You
I want to grow God
And I want to fall more in love with You
While growing

The Swell

It's not always about the swell
Soft keys begin the melody
Base chords, subtle, yet strong
Support the gentle keys.
The melody carries on with the constant
Hummmmm
Of the bass
The bass support fills in the side
The harmony joins
And it is beautiful.

The blending of the two tones
Bring a new meaning to a relationship
The duet, strong, yet…
Full of grace

And then you can feel it
Feel it in your chest
Feel it in your heart
Feel your feet tapping as the
melodies and harmonies swell
Build

All along He was working
But now you feel Him near
The build lessens
The swell flattens

And the harmony fades into the thick melody
Bass in the back

Always there
Supporting
Always leading

It's not always about the swell

Oh, My God

My God
Works out all things for His purposes
My God
Answers on His timing
My God
Turns broken into beautiful
My God is the Giver
Of endless grace and freedom

So, child of my God
Live in it.

As We Forgive Those

What does it look like
To forgive
To love
People who have hurt you?
People who oppose you?
What does it look like to pray
for
Someone
not about
someone?

The Widow
(*Mark 12:41–44 NIV*)

Shift our focus
Turn our eyes to You
Strip us of any idols
And pull us to You
Show us how to love
Not artificially but
Authentically
Show us how to give
Not the leftovers but
Everything we have
Shift our focus
So that You are the One
We treasure most

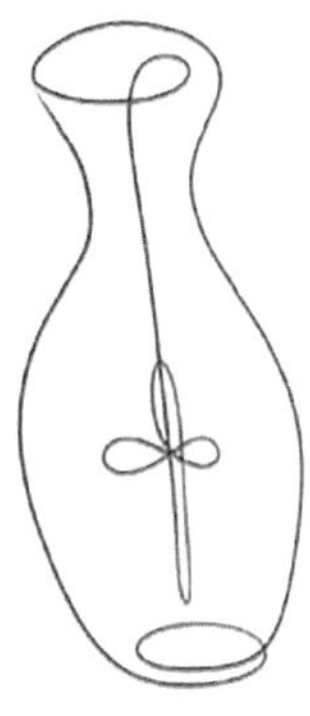

Morning Routine

Droplets of sweat
Nourishment
Twinkling of Christmas lights
Hot shower, hotter stove, hot tea—comforting
All of these things
I am grateful for
But I am most thankful

For Jesus.

Lord,
Your love showers me,
Let Your love pour over me forming
lasting droplets all over my heart,
Nourish me with Your fulfilling freedom,
Flow from the sweet aroma of Your love,
Let me walk in Your light,
Fill me with the comfort of Your Spirit

For You, I am most thankful.
All I need is You.

The Call

Knock! Knock! Knock!
Three raps on the door
Of my heart
"Are you listening, child?
I know you're there."

Open the door.

"I have saved you.
How will you respond?"

My first response:
Fear.

But I know what I want my response to be
What it should be:
Obedience.

Knock! Knock! Knock!
Three raps on the door
Of my heart
I reach for the door handle
And let a sliver of light
In.

Priorities

What are your priorities?
Grades, social life, health,
Faith?
Do they come before God?
What micro-idols
Soon to become large
Are sitting in my heart right now?

How can I say no,
So that I will grow?

Help My Unbelief
(Mark 9:24 NLT)

My fears
Are unbelief
When I fear about
Grad school
Finding a relationship
My friendships
Loss
I am choosing not to
Trust
Lord, I want to trust You
With every ounce of
My being
Replace my fears
With the comfort of Your grace
Replace my paralyzed senses
With eyes to see
Ears to hear
And a heart
To follow and trust
You

The Drinking Game

It's all a game
Of comparison
Who can be the funniest
Who can be the loudest
Who can be the prettiest
The more you drink
The more chances you have at winning

You become prettier
Funnier
Skinnier

But you don't.

It's all the lie
Of comparison
Your heart begins to follow other things
And you ask yourself

Who's winning now?

Love Languages

God,
You know our hearts,
You created them,
Help us to know one another's

I crave to know how to
Love well
Because how I want to be loved
Is not how my neighbor wants to be loved
Help me to love You
And understand
So I can love well.

My Yes

When You ask,
"Do you trust me?"
My answer is not always
Yes.
Let me let go of fleeting things
And hold onto You
So I can mean it
My yes.

her

I've never known a Love like Yours
You know the little things,
You know the details
So that I don't need to explain myself
But I can just be

I've never known a Love like Yours—
Pursuit, hospitality, challenging
Yet gentle
Like waves on a shoreline
You sweep over me, allowing me to sink deeper
And deeper
Into a Love that I can't explain

She doesn't know this Love yet
It is not human—no human could ever measure up

But she will

And when she does,
She will never know a Love like Yours

Active Listening

At whatever time of day I pray
I want to hear You
Even though I know every response is not
Always instant
I know that You are faithful
I know that You will answer
On Your terms—Your timing

So I trust
And I keep praying

Heart Canvas

Numb—I feel numb to it all

I don't know if it's a sign of
Weakness
Avoidance
Anger
Or peace
But I don't think it's the latter

I am weak, use my weakness as a canvas
For Your strength
Fill me with a peace that only comes from You

Because weakness feels like
Confusion
Chaos
A little heartache
And tears

Display Your strength in my heart
Here's my heart.

Not the First Rainbow, Nor the Last

A rainbow

On October 23
The day before my emotions took a hit
A reminder of Your faithfulness
Amidst so much hurt
Yet You ask for my
Yes
And even though it's difficult to utter

Yes.
I give it to You.
I give You control.

Breakup Breakthrough

Is he still thinking of me at this moment?
Do I still mean anything to him?
Did he learn anything about himself
during the time we spent together?
Was there anything between us, or was it all
in my head?

The answers to these questions are
Unknown
Chaotic
Overwhelming

But reworded…
The answers are
Constant.
Peaceful.
True.

Is He still thinking of me at this moment?
Do I still mean anything to Him?
Does He cause me to learn anything
during the time we spend together?

He says, "I delight in you."
And the answers are always
Yes and amen.

Check Please

He was a "same side of the table on a date guy"

Thumbs down.
So uncomfortable.

But we weren't always on the same side.
He didn't know what he wanted.

That was a thumbs down too.

So we moved to different sides.

The Snare of Comparison

Here we go again
Comparison.
It eats you alive
What you look like
Who's gonna care?
Are you independent enough?
Is money an issue?
How about the girl who could
Replace you.

God is bigger.
God is constant.
God is pursuing you.
God is patient.
For when you are anxious,
God is Love
God is the Potter

And you can't mold yourself.

Common Household Lie

"How are you?"
"Good, you?"

Why do I lie
When I'm not good?
I'm livid, frustrated,
OveRwhElmeD
But yet, I answer
"Good."

I'm busy, and it's getting
Out of hand
And the only thing I want to do
Is answer with the truth

Yet I continue to answer with a lie
"Good."
To not project my problems onto anyone else.

A Farmer's Market
(Romans 6:4b, 20–23)

gray, dull, a rotten stench fills the stall
laughter that crinkles your insides
with some enticing gimmicks
fruit flies buzz, close enough to touch

but

there's a barrier they can't cross

Into stalls with fullness
Of fruit
Blues, yellows, greens, reds, oranges
The brilliance is almost blinding
And the aroma that emanates
Fills the nostrils with a sweet, crisp sensation
Laughter that is filled with joy echoes

And the contrast is drastic.
Life
Or
death.

so why are you drawn to the flies?

Letter to the Editor

Ex-girlfriend
Dear "I don't know what I want,"
Do you still think about me?
Do you think the crisp air
is a little colder like I do?
When I sit like a shadow at my
family's table and watch
the couples laugh
and I think,
I'm the only single one.

Are the holidays hard for you
like they are for me?

Father
Dear "Waiting one,"
Where is your focus?
On the fact that you're still single,
Or on the fact that there is Someone
Who loves you greater than any human
Ever could?

Put your focus there, "Waiting one."

Free Indeed
(John 8:31–38 ESV)

Lord,
Do I look like I need to be set free?
My pride says
That I don't need You
My pride says
That I don't have to pray about
this, I've got it under control
When I face obstacles
I think, *How am I supposed to do this?*
But really, my pride blocks my way
Obscures my vision
Because in reality

I need You
My question should be reframed to
"How am I supposed to do this—
Without You?"

I want my interior to be cleansed by You
And my exterior to be free of embellishment

So that my pride is depleted
And You can shine through.

Strings Attached

I am a puppet on a string
I don't remember how I got here
I just remember the strings
Attaching themselves
One. By. One.
The string of pride on my foot
The string of technology on my finger

I didn't realize they were taking over

The string of perfection on my head
The string of people-pleasing on my lips
They continued to attach themselves
And I was overtaken

And now I sit
Not in control

In a state of "meh"
Spiritual apathy
Indifferent to what the Artist
Wants to do in my life

I was not created to be a puppet
To be attached to worthless things that are fleeting
I was not created to be apathetic
Unattach me, Lord
Pull me to You.

The Chase of Grace

You run to me with arms open wide

Even though I stray
Swerve toward earthly idols

God, reveal my idols and open my heart
Are they perfection, affection, attention,
technology, or acceptance?

What am I running toward
Instead of running toward Your grace?

There is no one like You
No one pursues my heart like You do
So why do I chase
Empty promises?

Lake Morning

Whoosh, whoosh
Gentle nothings of the waves and
wind fresh on my ears
I know You are here
You amaze me because You are so big
So constant
Yet You choose to speak to me
You have called me to this place
So use me, God
Every bit of me
I have been made for Your glory
So as broken as I am
Use me to bring
Love
To the people and places
Where darkness rests
Use me, God.
I am Yours.

Prayer for Her

She goes to the water too
That's where she finds peace
I can relate—but I know where the
Source of my peace is

Help her to find that Source
Let the water that ripples lightly
Flow like living rivers into her heart
Open her heart so that You may flow in

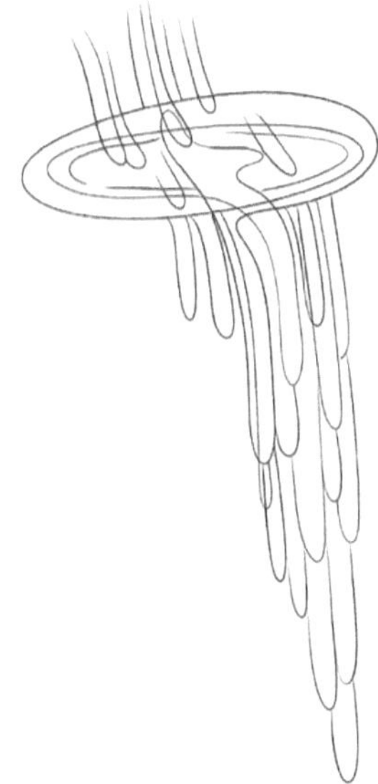

Through Him
(Philippians 4:4–13 ESV)
"I can do all things through him
who strengthens me."

Where I am weak,
You are strong
When I am anxious
You bring peace
(Peace that even I cannot understand)
When I worry
You remind me to be thankful
You remind me to think of every
good thing that You give
Like Your strength

Thank You, Lord,
Be strong
Be peace in my heart
Today.

Glory in the Morning

In the stillness—my heart is calmed
Just like the water where the sun
Reflects Your love
The water glistens and calls me
Deeper
My squinty eyes, looking, searching
I lean in to see Your goodness
I lean in to listen for Your call—through the birds
The tiny bugs, the simple splashes in front of me
The rays of the sun fan out in a
glorious display, and I am in awe
Of You
Lord, never let this awe be fleeting,
never let the wonder leave my eyes

You are all around me
Your breath
In everything I do
I say
I see

I want to be obedient—I want more of this
More of You

Downpour

The rain pours hard
Pitter-patter, pitter-patter
But
Your love pours harder
I long for someone to love
But
You've put people right in front of me
To love them as You do
To love the little pieces of heaven
You've placed on earth
To see Your heart, Lord,
To feel Your heart break
Show me how to love
So that I can feel You
The rain is pouring harder
Still.
Your love pours harder

Bike Ride
(Psalm 139:13–14 ESV)

Gravel crunches underneath my tires
Pedal faster. You need to have thinner legs!
But in front of you
Is your dad,
Behind you, your mom
They are proud
Beside you,
The glass reflection that shimmers in the lake,
Each sparkle a promise
From your Father,
"I have made you,
I love you"

Gravel crunches underneath my tires
I know I am loved from all sides

Take-Out

Isn't it funny?
How a drawer full of crinkled take-out menus
Represents our life?
How we have the option to choose
what we want to order
When we want to order it
But,
(there's always a but)
We can't choose absolutely anything we want
Only
What's on the menu
We are limited to what's on the menu
Yet,
We serve a limitless God

So why do you turn to crinkled menus that have
Limits
When you can close that drawer

And choose a limitless One instead?

Strangers in a Flea Market

When I walk through a flee market,
There are so many journeys that
I don't know
But I choose not to make eye contact
I avoid them, why?

Because I am in a hurry
Wanting to go where
I
Want to go
Not stopping, pausing
To love them
To look into their eyes and see their story

Turtle Alley

Silently,
The turtle sits on the log
Breathing in the warmth of the afternoon sun
Almost every turtle stretches
One arm up
And tilts its head toward the
Warmth Giver
With a gaping stare

I like to think of us
The Church
As turtles

Waiting for warmth
Stretching out our hands
So God can touch us
Mouths open wide in awe
Awe of the light our Father sheds on us daily
We don't deserve His grace
But He gives it
Freely
Daily
Just like the sun shines

If we aren't thinking like the turtles yet
We should be.

Loss of Signal

Dead spots
You know they're coming
But refuse to believe they're there
Good conversation, life bringing wo—
Cut off
In the dead space.

You'd think we'd be ready for them
For the moments when all communication
Seems lost
But they come out of nowhere
Disconnecting us
Leaving us longing to return

To Life-giving communication.

Temple Care

Mirrors are the enemy
So is Instagram
But yet…
You stare at these things daily
Wondering why your legs aren't thinner

Your body is a temple
So you eat healthy
Run (sometimes)
And try to take care of it
But are you taking care of the temple for God

Or for yourself?

Do you want to look good?
Feel better?
Or use your one shell on earth for Him?

Most days, I'd answer with
The selfish option.

Autumn

When I wake up,
Lord, I want You to be the first thing
I crave
I want to need You
Like I can't breathe without You
Fill my lungs with Your breath

As the leaves fall
And the air becomes crisp
Let my whole body cry out
As the earth does when the
Seasons change.

Let my life be a reflection
Of Your beauty
Just like the leaves
From green
To red, orange, yellow, brown
And when the sun hits them

They radiate

Help me radiate
When the Son hits me.

Watercolor in the Park

Watercolor
It's a forgiving art
Room to change, contrast
Lighten, darken

Let my heart be the
Art
Of watercolor
Forgiving
Full of peace
Gentle

Yet creative
Passionate
Deep.

Still, My Yes

Let there be
Nothing
I hold onto

All of these things I place in Your hands.

When you asked, "Do you trust me?"
My answer was not initially, "Yes."
My answer is not always, "Yes."
Let me trust You.
Let me hold onto You

And not these things.

Traffic Light Worship

Broken lights flash red
Slowing slower stop
Nowhere to go
But to You with a halleluiah
Nowhere to be
But in Your Presence
In the front seat of my car
A mundane stop at a traffic light
But a prime front-row seat
To worship the Father

Identity Math

Numbers.
Why do 3 numbers
Seem 2 define me
When only 1 should
Why do I live 2 achieve the extremes
High numbers
Low numbers
When I should live 2
Witness
2 many people

Why does everyone around me
Tell me my numbers
Aren't good enough
When my identity is found in 1
And 1 only

Why are your GPA and the scale running your life
when the high King of Heaven
should be?

The Vine
(John 15:1–11 ESV)

My heart longs for
Home
Longs to
Abide
Somewhere where my identity is
Known
Somewhere where someone
Believes in me
Pours into me
Where I am
Chosen

But I am pulled in different directions
Labels define me
And I walk in
Circles
Searching for life
A path

To walk

With someone

Someone who knows my
Name.

So will I listen to that call…
"Follow me."
The call to
Abide.

Will I follow?
Will I allow change?
Allow myself to be
Known.

The Court

"us" versus "them"
A competition engrained in our hearts
From day one

We are trained and coached to defend ourselves
Defend the "us"
And don't let "them" score
Like a basketball defender, hunger
blazing in their eyes
To stop the "them"

It is in this mentality that
Pride, untruth, and division
Fester

But what if instead of blocking "them"
We stopped playing defense

And we learned from "them"
Evaluating "us"
What if we listened to "them"
And unstuck ourselves from our "us" ways

What if we were unified?

We Are Paul
(Philippians 1:3–7 ESV)

Paul was imprisoned.
A great disgrace.
But his partners in the gospel
Never left his side.

God, our faithful God
Never left his side.

He was filled with joy
Encouragement
And faith-filled prayers.

We are all Paul.

Imprisoned in our struggles.
Disgraces to ourselves, maybe others
But we are also a team.
Partners.
And we have one thing in common.

We serve a faithful God.

So, God,
Thank You for never leaving,
Fill us with joy,
Let us march on together
Partners
Linking arms
To further Your Kingdom.

SkIN Condition

My hands hurt
They are cracked and breaking
From washing them.
But, God,
Is this how it feels when You begin to cleanse us?

You break us.
And use our brokenness
To heal others

So, God,
As I wash my hands
Help me, in turn, to wash feet
To wash the feet of those around me.

Revive our nation
Quench our dry hands
And lands.

Show us Your Light
In this darkness
There is a war going on and
We are fighting
But You already won.

So as I wash my hands
Use my cracks to heal those around me

You break to grow new skin, new life.

Search My Heart

It's okay to cry
Especially when you lose something
But is it okay to cry

When you asked for it?

When you asked God
To search your heart?

He found the holes.
Let Him fill them.

Pandemic Song

The world was broken
Our idols silenced
Empty hearts searching for you

The world was grieving
Loss of material things
Empty hearts searching for You

But that's when You broke through
Your light shone through the dark
You spoke through the silence
You pulled on our hearts

O God,
You are my refuge
The One I run to
You alone
O God, You're the Giver of Life
And the only One to
Satisfy my soul

The void seemed deep
My strength was weak
But You called me to my knees

You said,
"The only way to fight your way through is if

You let Me fight for you."

But that's when You broke through
Your light shone through the dark
You spoke through the silence
You pulled on our hearts

O God,
You are my refuge
The One I run to
You alone
O God, You're the Giver of Life
And the only One to
Satisfy my soul

You break to rebuild
You make brokenness whole
You see our ugly hearts
Yet You make them beautiful
You take away our idols
And You take their place
You rip away fears
So that we might have faith

You said,
"The only way to fight your way through is if
You let Me fight for you."

Thoughts Turning to Tears

I feel tears welling up in the back of my eyes
Don't ask me why.
I maybe just feel overwhelmed
Stuck
Confused
Out
Of
Control.

Take my tears and anxieties

I know that You are in control.
Let that sink in.

I know that You are in control.

Guide me to surrender
Because You
Are the only One who
Knows my heart
And knows what is going to happen.

Silence my thoughts
And turn my attention
Pull my heart
To You.

Rekindling Zeal

Ignite.
Extinguish the toxic complacency
I feel like I'm living a monotonous life
And my heart isn't passionate
About anything

Usually, I am passionate
About
Jesus
Learning
My family
Pursuit of community
Reading
Coffee.

But it all seems a bit distant
A bit meh.

Reignite my passions
My passion to love others
To serve You
To grow
To learn

Remove this toxic complacency
And replace it with a zeal for You
That infiltrates every area of my life

Winter Dust

Snow-covered trees
Slight signs of burnt orange still peaking
Squirrels scurry making snow dust fall
Lightly
From atop the trees
Magical.

Holy Spirit dust over us today
Fall lightly like the snow
When we move, scurry
Let us do so with intention
To let You cover us
And make life more than
Magical.

Fulfilled.

Grandpa

"You're the life of the party"
He said.
As he is about to have the
Party of a lifetime

No more oxygen tanks
No more Covid
No more pokes, prods

Just Jesus.

Be...

Be everything for everyone
Be busy, hustling, and bustling
Be perfect, act like you have it all together
Be yourself, put on a face
So you look like you're strong

But in order to "just be"
You can't be all these things.

The Night Before

The Christmas lights twinkle
And here I sit
Staring
In between the lights
That seem dull
In my numbness

I don't know what to feel
I am tired, sad, empty
And deep down
I know
God is faithful
And I've seen His faithfulness

And yet,
When I don't get a moment to
myself to process it all
It all seems so overwhelming

And sadly,
The Christmas lights feel dull
In this season.

The Morning After

Stillness.
The pink skies whisper His power in
the wispy nature of the clouds
Frozen in time, small ripples in the pond
In awe at the glistening beauty
Calling to the onlooker to
Rest
As the other half of the pond
Gently beckons the onlooker
Into the day

But slowly,
Take time to marvel
This is anything but
Dull
And it awakens the heart
To rejoice
Rest
Receive
The One who made it all.

The water, once a dull gray
Now a bright pink
Reflecting the cotton candy sky of the morning

Just as the onlooker reflects the Creator

Heart of Worship

The same feels new again,
When the Spirit falls fresh
Lyrics hundreds of years old
Sung many times over
Can impact a heart

Each time

If you let it.

Luke 2:19

And Mary pondered all these things

In her heart

All the small moments,
Smiles
Innocent childlike prayers with eyes peeking open
Sweet bites of dessert fighting through fullness
Two-dollar bills
Naps on the couch
Cuddles from littles

All of these small things to ponder
About Christmas

To treasure every moment
Because this is the first Christmas
Without Grandpa.

The Heart of God

…is curious
Questioning
Discerning
Instead of shuffling through "how it's always been,"
A comfortable, yet dangerous place to stay,

The heart of God is curious
Searching for answers
Making the clear, muddy
The black-and-white, gray

Yet bringing clarity into the picture
Through open-minded understanding
Thought-provoking questions
That cause us to step into the uncomfortable
And grow.

Homecoming

How will I
Respond?
How will I combat these feelings
that are not of You?
Feelings of loneliness, impatient doubt,
And guilt.

Not of You.

But I will respond with
Gratitude.

Lord, today,
Let my heart be grateful
Fill me with celebration
The celebration You make when
A sheep is found
When Your child
Comes home.

And Your celebration cancels out all
guilt, loneliness, impatient doubt.
Because You are Home.

Heart Broken

Break my heart for what breaks
Yours
Let the hurt around me
Not go unnoticed
Let us shift our eyes
Let us live with a
Gospel mindset

Humble me, God.

Help my life to reflect Yours
A life of
Radical love

A life that says,
Not for my own glory
But for Yours.

Teach me to hate injustice
Teach me to crave
You
Show me how You bring beauty from ashes

Lord, I know You are hurting
Because Your people are hurting.

So break my heart
For what breaks Yours.

Prodigal
(Luke 15:11–32 NLT)

If repentance hurts
Then why is it freeing?

Because He is
Running
To you—
Against everything culture says,
"You're unworthy"
"You're guilty"
"You will never bounce back from this"
"What have you done?"

Yet—
He runs.
To you.

When you return to Him.

And in that brokenness, in the waiting
There is hope.
A celebration in the return.

So let my heart return to You, Father.

I don't want to live without Your Presence,
Without Your celebration.

A Season of Waiting

Expectant wait—it is active in nature,
Yet can be exhausting.

But asking for faith
For a deep hope in a promise
Gives us stamina,
Endurance.
Like a mother waits for a child to be born
Living in the tension of bringing
a child into the world
Yet the reward of raising a human
with the Holy Spirit inside
Or a future bride waiting for a husband, for
the deep intimacy of knowing someone
Yet living into the deeper trust that the covenant
of God's marriage to her heart is far greater
Like the tide waiting for the right time to turn
Bringing shells to the shore as a reminder
of our broken beauty in the waves,
In the waiting.
So let my expectant heart nearly
burst for joy at Your pursuit,
For returning to You in the waiting is far greater.

Prayer for the Present

Your Kingdom is here
Right now
Yesterday
Tomorrow

Today.

In my midst.
So let my heart sing for joy
Along with creation

Today.

I may not understand how
You are working
But
You are working
Have worked
And will continue to work
In my life.

Today.

Kingdom Pursuit

If it doesn't further Your Kingdom
I don't want it.

If his pursuit doesn't mirror Yours,
I don't want it.

Glimpses of Your love were displayed
Through human love,
But then they weren't.
Because he was human.

So if the way he talks to me
Doesn't mirror the way You speak to me
I don't want it.

And if it doesn't further Your Kingdom,
I don't want it.

I want what You want—even if
it hurts in the process.

Collateral Damage

Sometimes that's what it feels like
When God is using you to push someone else
in the direction that He is leading them

A causality
That you may never understand
But one that God used and is continuing to use

So in the middle of the, "Why God?"
"Why me?"
"Why did I have to be the one who was
hurt in the process of their growing?"

Trust.

Because maybe you're growing too.
In this season
Of being collateral damage.

"Fickle"

"Feelings are fickle,"
They don't last,
Yet feelings are
Valid.
Real.

Are feelings the cornerstone that
relationships are built upon?
Absolutely not—
Deceit.
Wavering.
Confusing.
Because if they were…

The relationship would be sinking sand.

But is Jesus Christ the cornerstone?
Absolutely.

Full of love.
Solid.
True.

But Jesus felt too.
And His feelings were real, valid.

Yet,
He was firm, solid, true.

Doors

I'll keep asking God
And if You hold the door because
there's a fire on the other side
I'll keep knocking
I'll keep seeking
And maybe You'll open
Another.

The Muffler
(Isaiah 43:2 ESV)

I thought it would scar
The burn
Remnants of him
(and his motorcycle)
Etched in my skin

And it did.
But only for a little while.

With time,
And truth
New skin grew
And it did not consume
But rather
Faded
Into a part of my story
Etching into my heart

An initial burn
But a deeper
Trust.

Matthew 7:7–8

You say,
"Take heart"
Keep asking, keep knocking, seeking,

Right now, I feel as if I am
Pounding

And there are some doors open
But just a crack
And I feel as if they could slam at any moment

And others are
Closed.

Slammed shut for the protection
Of my heart.

But the slamming hurt.

And maybe I trust people too easily.

When really the harder thing to do
Is to trust You.

Less Rest

I can't stop crying
It's like a well that never ends
Where are these tears coming from?

I just feel so ~~wrestless~~ **restless**
Like I don't know what to do
With myself

But maybe my spelling error
Wasn't an error

I am wrestling with this brokenness
Trying to be present
But wrestling with broken hopes
And ultimate questions

Wrestling with this "temporary"

Gardens

Growth.
Why does it take so much
Breaking
Uprooting
Change

To be rooted
Planted?

The Things of God
(Mark 8:33 ESV)

What I want
Is not always what You plan
What I want
Is not of God, it's of (wo)man
What I want
Is for things to make sense
What I want
Is not always how Your plans commence

What You want
Is for me to have life
Even if that means there'll be some
Sorrow and strife

What You want
Is better than I can even think

It might not make sense
But that's the mystery
The beauty
Of what You want.

Adulting

Why does adulting feel like a stomachache?
The "what-ifs" churning
But peace, still
Yet
Why does adulting feel like
I want to cry
And need a nap
But also want to run and leap
For joy
All at the same time?

Is adulting always this confusing?

Now I see why Jesus called us
To have faith like
Children
Who live in simplicity

Turn my chaos
Into sweet simplicity
Turn my adulting into
Sincere and innocent
Joy
Full of wisdom and trust.

Resurrection Day
(*John 20:11–18*)

What was it like when He uttered,
"It is finished"
When darkness spread over the world
Did darkness cover the earth?
Did all hope feel lost?
Did the enemy feel a tease of victory,
Even though he knew in the back of
his head he had lost anyway?

But when Jesus rose
Did the sun feel just a bit brighter?
Did Satan tremble?
And did the birds sing a little bit louder?
Did breakfast smell a little bit sweeter?
Did the earth look a lush green,
greener than the day before?

Or were the people too caught up
in their own grief to notice
The victory of the Lord?

But then

He said her name.
And her eyes opened, she saw
The world became sweeter
Grief melted with one word
"Mary"

When He says your name
Do your eyes light up with wonder?
With intimate knowing
That you are alive
Because He is alive.

Descendant Elevator

Tears fall along with the elevator
7—I feel frustrated
6—I am not seen
5—More tears
4—I'm not heard
3—Pull yourself together, the doors will open in
2—They expect you to uphold a standard
1—I white knuckle it and hold onto
"I'm fine."

Cherished

When I feel unseen
You see me.
When I feel like everything is changing
You don't. You are constant.
When I feel like I deserve an apology
I remember Your grace.
When I try to move fast
You tell me to slow down,
Breathe.
When I need a hug,
You embrace me.

Thank You, Father.

Waves

Excited squeals of joy
Come
The waves come
Consider it joy
When waves come your way…

Why would I do that?
Hitting a wall of water
Feels like you're drowning

But the children love the thrill,
They wait with expectant excitement
At each rolling wave

The waves make us stronger
So why don't you squeal with excitement
Like the children

When the waves come.

2 Corinthians 3

If I am a letter
Written so that people may hear Your
Name
Let the words written on my heart
Reflect You entirely
I want others to know that
In You
There is freedom
I want others to feel Your
Love
Just as I have

Help me to be a letter
Daily
Your gospel written on my heart

Snail mail is a sweet surprise.
The gospel is even sweeter.

VDay

flowers, chocolate, frills, and lace
splashes of pinks and reds

ways to express sweet love.

but an even sweeter love
was expressed through
humanity
death
flowing of reds
resurrection
Victory
grace.

so how do you express your love
to a Lover who gave
everything…

not just a few bucks on chocolate?

Sukkah[*]

A booth or hut roofed with branches, built
against or near a house or synagogue and
used during the Jewish festival of Sukkoth
as a temporary dining or living area.[†]

Leave your luxuries behind
The comforts that you grow fond of
Made you drift into complacency

Walk away
Go

Live in a sukkah
Remember the desert
For this
This is where you experience the profound
Tangible
Celebratory
Presence of God

Our luxuries blind us
Telling us to lie to ourselves
About who we are

---

[*] "Sukkah," accessed May 10, 2023, https://www.dictionary.com/browse/sukkah.

[†] *Rod VanSolkema, "Feasts of Tabernacles—Sukkot," Crossroads Bible Church, 23 September 2018, Grand Rapids, MI. Sermon.*

But the desert
Cultivates vulnerability
The desert flaunts your flaws
And this is where you
Thrive
This is where you will grow

And here
In the midst of the uncomfortable
You will find comfort, celebration
In the sukkah.

The Well (John 4:1–45)

O searching heart, you seek
And find
Temporary fulfillment
Temporary joy

But there is something greater
O searching heart

Find nourishment
Fulfillment
In the One
Who searches hearts.

Not a Cinderella Story[*]
(2 Kings 18–19)

Hilary Duff once said,
"Because waiting for you is like waiting
for rain in this drought…"

Droughts are when things are
Dry
Realizing the deep need for rain
Grasping the vital action
Of asking

It is hard to keep asking
When you don't see
To keep working tirelessly
As Diner Girl

But often
Listen closely
Pitter-patter, pitter-patter
Far on the horizon
Like a whisper
Coming to shower and bring fresh life
Into dry, desert hearts

---

[*] Mark Rosman, *A Cinderella Story,* (United States: Warner Bros.) 2004.

We just need to listen for the whisper of rain
And wait.

Because faith isn't always a Cinderella story

Rainfall

Watching the rain
From afar
As it pours out the gaping gap in the clouds

It's like taking the perspective
Of the author of this poem
Just days earlier

As the rain poured hard
She felt it
Heard the intense pattering
On her car windows

But now seeing it from afar
It looks so gentle

Necessary for growth.

And She Stayed

Stay.
It seems like a passive word.
To sit.
Wait.
Be still.

But staying means to
Grow
Relationships
Comfort levels
Fruit.

So as passive as it seems
Staying is an
Active response.

Street Lamps

The street lamps are just floating bulbs of light
On this dark morning
The only source of light as I wait
For the sun to rise
And illuminate my little cul-de-sac
But until then

I wait.

I watch the little bulbs
Bright as they can be
Shining only on what's in front of them

And isn't that what You're asking me to do
Wait for the glorious illumination
But in the meantime

Focus on what's directly in front of me?

The morning crickets chime in their agreement.

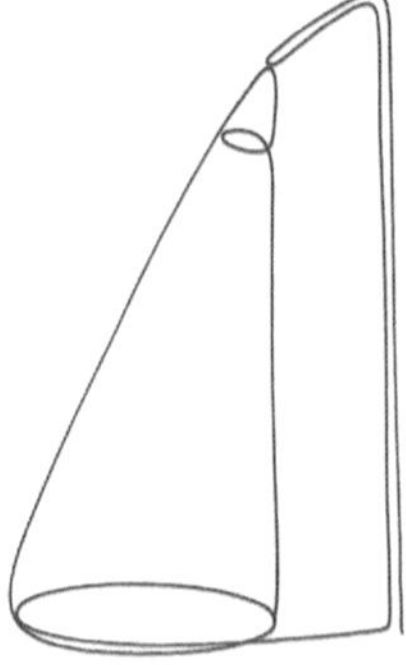

Proverbs 4

Let me be attentive
To Your Words
I don't want to miss a thing
If I turn my eyes

Away

I am apt to stumble
But when I keep my eyes

Forward

You guide me
With Your bright light
With wisdom
Let me be attentive
Hanging onto every Word
Because You are the Giver of

Life

Isn't that where I want my attention to be?

Long-Distance Friends

We see the same sunrise
Although miles away
And though the sunrise
Doesn't close the gap of distance
We serve the same God
Of peace
Who can fill the gaps even we
thought were too large

So, God of peace,
Provide a sense of nearness
To the scattered people

Who see the same sunrise

Awaken My Soul

An extra cup of coffee on a Thursday morning
Needed to keep my eyes
Awake

But, Lord, let my heart be
Awake
Always
Let it seek the only "caffeine" it needs
You.

So maybe I am drinking an extra cup
To keep my body awake

But let my heart,
Let it remain awake
Searching for You in every moment.

Prepositions

Prepositions matter.

God is…

With.
In.
Through.
Before.
By.
Beside.

You.

Small words.
Vast meaning.

The Preposition WITH

Expecting people to understand the word
"with"
Is like trying to keep a snowflake
Forever
"In the same direction as…"[*]
"Accompanied by…"[†]

Each other?

But are we always moving
In the same direction as each other?
Are you accompanied by the
Same
Humans through every journey?

No.

But you are accompanied by the same God.
And He understands the word
with

God is with us.
In step with us.
In and through the storms.
And is the constant
Accompaniment.

---

[*]   dictionary.com.

[†]   Ibid.

"How much more"
Will I worry about my appearance?
"How much more"
Will I hold onto success so tightly
That my fingers feel as if they will fall
off from the loss of circulation?
"How much more"
Will I go on anxiously measuring life by
Calories
Friends
Time-ticking singleness?

Yet, "how much more"
Does He provide
What you cannot,
In the exact moment you need?

"How much more" will He give when you
Ask, trust
From your heart?

"How much more" will He provide because
"How much more" valuable are you
Than a sparrow?

Genesis 15–18

Crisp autumn air brings
Color changes
In the leaves

But someone once told me that some leaves
Change color sooner than the crispness of fall arrives
Sooner than the cooling of the temperature
Because they are under

Stress

Brings about an urge to quickly change
Seasons
In humans, too
Although we may not be ready yet

Like Abram and Hagar
Trying to change plans on
Human time
When God's timing was much

Better
Fuller

Are the leaves, colors of fall
When they change on time

Not rushing because of stress
But allowing the color change to
Slowly take place
Take over the green of summer
And metamorphose into fall

All the while
Waiting patiently
For a few degrees to drop

So the leaves can, too.

A Question

Maybe I should stop asking
Maybe?
Maybe this is why…

Why.

You don't need to know it
Just trust.

Maybe I just need courage.

"Courage, dear heart"[*]

It takes courage to trust and obey
But being courageous
Cannot be compared

It looks differently for every heart.

I've seen courage in the tears of a broken heart
Choosing to continue to dream and ask God
For something better
I've seen courage in a mother's tenacity
Choosing to raise her child with strength and love
Despite patterns of unfaithfulness
I've seen courage in the heart of an athlete
Pushing through the difficult days
When training was a mountain

And this is faith—
Take courage, dear heart.

---

[*] C. S. Lewis, *The Voyage of the Dawn Treader* (Wyatt North Publishing, LLC) 2002.

Chasing the Sunrise

A little sliver, just a sliver
Erupts into a great blinding light
Purples, oranges, pinks, blues, every
beautiful color you can imagine
From just a small sliver, a small sliver that
you didn't expect would erupt into
Something beautiful.

But you must keep chasing it.

Intimate Communication

Whisper prayers
Are the prayers that when they roll off your tongue,
They mean the most
Barely audible,
Yet heard.

Whisper prayers are the
Breath prayers
That are deepest in your heart
The ones you know you're holding onto,
and you need to give to God,

But sometimes
Whisper prayers are the hardest to utter
Because if you mean it,
God will use it

Because He listens closely

And communicates through whispers, too

Psalm 8:3–4

There has been a shift toward
A mindfulness movement
Be present in the details
Notice
Your breath
Breathe
Awareness back into your soul
Recenter, delight
In your senses

But mindfulness
Has been around since the
Beginning
When God spoke the universe into
Existence

He is mindful of the

details

Of you.

He breathes life into you
He is present
In every moment
He attends to every detail, He
Delights

In you.
And God Who created the entirety of the universe
Full of exploding color, fresh wind,
warmth (and lack thereof)

Is mindful of you.

What are we that You are mindful of us?

Conversations with the Heart of God

So often, the Spirit speaks through us
Yet we don't even know it.

But usually, it's God preparing our hearts
As we have conversations with His.

To live in freedom,
Is to live in the gospel
And it is simple
Yet we make it to be complicated

But to live
Truly live
Is to have conversations
With the Heart of God
With His people.

And then,
To listen.

Epilogue

And in these "conversations"
Often held over a
Cup of coffee
Is where my words were stirred
And where
Jesus
Remained.

About the Author

Malinda Lugbill is a young professional who grew up in a small rural town in Ohio. She graduated from Calvin University where she earned her master's degree in speech-language pathology. She currently works as a speech-language pathologist, but when she's not working, she loves being active, preferably outside. Malinda enjoys a good cup of coffee surrounded by people she loves and hopes you can do the same as you use her words to reflect, listen, and grow deeper in a relationship with Jesus.

9 7 9 8 8 8 9 4 3 8 3 8 0